SAUL

THE MIRACLE ON THE ROAD

Copyright © 1997 Carine Mackenzie
ISBN: 978-1-85792-296-7
Reprinted 2000, 2002, 2004, 2007, 2010 and 2015
Published by Christian Focus Publications, Geanies House,
Fearn, Tain, Ross-shire, IV20 1TW, Scotland, U.K.
www.christianfocus.com
Printed in China

Saul was born in Tarsus, in the country that we now call Turkey. His parents were Jewish and young Saul was brought up to learn the law of God in great detail.

When he was young, his parents sent him to Jerusalem to study under the famous teacher Gamaliel. He was a keen student and lived an upright life.

When he grew up he became a teacher of the Jewish law, a rabbi. He also learned the trade of a tentmaker. Saul was a clever man.

Saul was a strict religious law-keeper. He hated the Christian people who were growing in number. They were people who trusted in the Lord Jesus Christ. They believed that he had died for their sins and followed his teaching.

Saul did all he could to hurt the Christian people.

When many people were throwing stones at Stephen because he told them about Jesus, Saul looked on in approval. He even took care of their belongings.

He hated Jesus and all the people that followed him. But Saul was going to change!

Saul, with an official letter of permission, set off for Damascus. His plan was to find any man or woman who was following the Lord Jesus and arrest them. Then he would take them back to Jerusalem to be punished or even killed. Saul's heart was full of hatred.

As he came near to Damascus around midday, suddenly a bright light shone from heaven. Saul threw himself on the ground, terrified. He heard a voice saying, 'Saul, Saul, why are you persecuting me?'

Saul answered, 'Who are you, Lord?'

The voice replied, 'I am Jesus of Nazareth whom you are persecuting. It is dangerous for you to fight against my power.'

The people with Saul saw the light and were very afraid.

Saul was trembling with fear too.

'What do you want me to do?' he asked.

'Get up and go to the city of Damascus and there you will be told what to do,' the Lord replied.

Saul rose from the ground. When he opened his eyes, he found that he could not see. The dazzling bright light had blinded him.

He was led by the hand on the rest of the journey to Damascus, and taken to the house of Judas in Straight Street.

For three days Saul ate and drank nothing. He was completely blind. He spent time praying to God. God heard his prayers and sent someone to help him.

Ananias, a follower of the Lord Jesus, lived in Damascus. God spoke to him in a vision.

'Go to Straight Street, to Judas' house and ask for a man called Saul from Tarsus. He is praying there.'

Ananias was nervous. 'I have heard about that man, Lord,' he said. 'He has done a lot of harm to your people in Jerusalem. He has permission to come here to arrest those who follow you.'

'Go!' the Lord reassured him, 'I have chosen him to preach about me to all sorts of people.'

Ananias found Saul where God had told him.

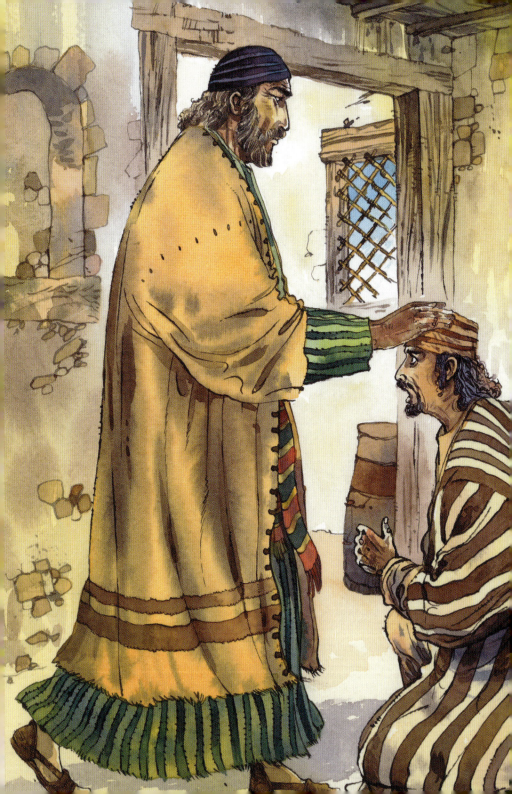

'Brother Saul,' he said. 'The Lord Jesus who spoke to you on the road here, has sent me to you so that you may receive your sight back. You will be filled with the Holy Spirit too.'

Immediately something like scales fell from Saul's eyes and he could see again.

Saul was baptised to show that he was now a believer in the Lord Jesus Christ. He had begun a new life. He then ate a good meal which gave him strength.

The believers in Damascus welcomed Saul. He preached about Jesus in the synagogues, passing on the good news that Jesus is the Son of God.

Saul preached so powerfully in Damascus, that the Jews were very upset. Eventually, they plotted together to kill Saul. Saul heard about this wicked plot. He would have to escape. The Jews set guards on watch at all the gates of the city; they wanted to be sure to catch Saul.

The believers (now Saul's friends) made a good plan. They got hold of a large basket. Saul slipped inside it and his friends carefully let the basket down by ropes over the city wall. In this way Saul made his escape.

In Jerusalem, the followers of Jesus were afraid when Saul tried to join them. They remembered how cruel he had been when he was in Jerusalem. They could hardly believe that he was a different man.

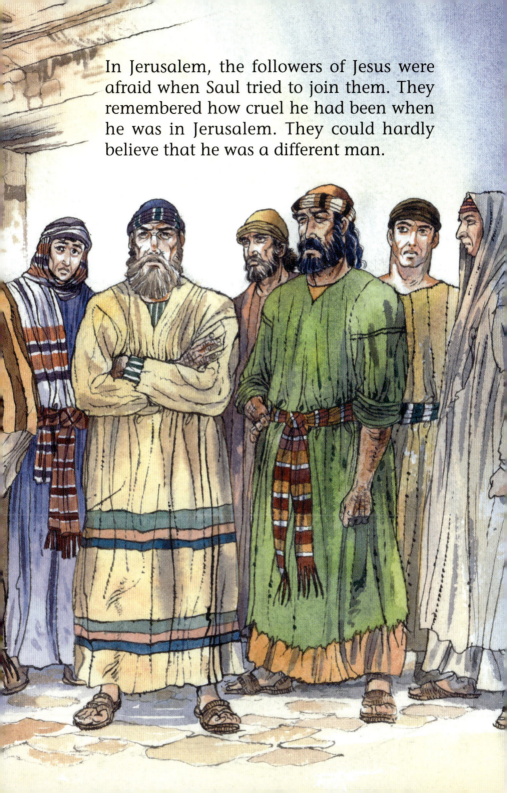

A kind man called Barnabas spoke up for Saul. 'He has really changed. The Lord Jesus met him on the road to Damascus. He has preached boldly already in Damascus about the Lord.'

The Christians then gladly accepted him as their friend and brother.

What a change in the life of Saul! What had made the difference? The dramatic meeting with the Lord Jesus Christ was the turning point in Saul's life. Saul later wrote: 'Jesus Christ came into the world to save sinners – of whom I am the worst. But I was shown mercy.'

Jesus is still meeting with sinners. In his Word, the Bible, he tells us that we too can receive the same mercy and forgiveness that Saul did by trusting in Jesus alone.